THE ASSASSINATION
OF
COLOUR

ELDON GRIER

Fiddlehead Poetry Books, 1978

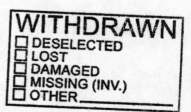

Grier, Eldon, 1917-
  The assassination of colour

(Fiddlehead poetry books; 231)

Poems.

ISBN 0-920110-60-6 pa.

I. Title. II. Series.

PS8513.R54A87   C811'.5'4   C77-001808-4
PR9199.3.G75A87

CONTENTS

MEXICO CITY HOTEL GENEVE APRIL 1970

most of us welcome machines that make steady granular noises
or roaring ingest the air on ocean voyages or at the back of
darkened motels
the drains that slip our nightly messages bring stillness up
and sleep
like the bursting out of flowers. . .

here I am awake and locked inside a brown and white colonial
set
my isolation is a must of blue policemen (the rifleman I never was)
the wind a tower placing tokens on my eyes   the coolness close
to violence
in its intervention. . .

and

I've finally met a clever Mexican ironist
a Toronto educated orthodontist
    as his wife was too
you (he laughed) Canadians are funny
funny yes and desperate said I
AND YOU SHOULD BE TOO

    we both fell bleeding onto the heap
    the fate of all
    good planners in sadness

2.

    a winter evening
nineteen forty-five the bus at rest
emptied of its bottled life bombarded
by a day and night of travelling
old curves catching up like boomerangs
pot-holes from the road outside Victoria

how I loved this place! the feeling of some brown accelerator
locked to the floor fed by the movements of blood
the smell of dryness chemical-natural-seminal

the sky with its
hypo of blue
pitiful palms like the musty dresses in a museum
dresses curving the streets in steady migrations

        and the "Dali" character
        who gave us a home
        Italo d'Andrea dressed
        in his purple turtleneck
        and bowler hat or in his
        purple silk-lined cape
                there too
        was blond and swollen Betty
        Carmen from Santa Barbara made motherly
        by her hard experience
        Ron the gentle fugitive from justice
        Henry horse-faced poet
        from Amsterdam I was
        the innocent one the straightman
        I paid the rent

and there was a parrot who sang soprano
and who'd cry PAPA YO TENGO FRIO
when the clear black shade
started climbing in his cage

and the pair of medical students who probed
our minor infections like comic gardeners

joven!
si!
    joven
     joven
      joven

and
    I haven't forgotten the night you clawed me
    down the back
    screaming hysterical too much spitting
    too much burning contact unregenerate noise
    gonorrhoea in the flabby
    singing faces children hustlers

limbless bodies
grinning turtles
moving in your wake

    ah the horror of it all

did you know that in nineteen forty-five almost all the city
                  buses had holes in their mufflers and
did you know that in that year several teachers were killed in
                  the great crusade against ANALFABETISMO
did you know that just behind the Zocalo there was a revolutionary circle pledged to the immediate overthrow of the
                  Guatemalan government
did you know that I read the name of Igor Gouzenko on the
                  second page of the Grafica Noticias
and I knew in terrible loss that PEACE was a word for children
                  to play with   a lullaby

3.

joven   joven

       things have changed
       the gap remains the same

   however

dust remembers water and its dense authority
glyph reshapes the pot   the bug-eyed entity comes
streaming rain across the tortured evenings almost
unrecognized by lovers   almost unchecked
by the clay-faced police
the city's lost momentum is notably our gain
the parked volcanoes shine as dully as a tourist brochure
the frantic cars decelerate with speed
yoked to a full-length portrait of Malinche

MEXICO SIQUEIROS RIVERA 1945

AMBIENTE PARTICULAR

the first time
I saw the volcanoes I
was walking away
from the last bus stop
in the Lomas de Chapultepec
nothing prepared me for
their position in the sky
such mythic structures
on and of the land

the Mexican nation also
appeared as a volcano
an upthrust of people
its peak above the level
and distant strata of abstract ideas
its reality a fact even
in the blackouts of power
the dust storms of a largely
organic evolution

a claiming and unfolding both
backward and forward

SUMMER FOR SURE

summer for sure   like an Aztec serpent an
orange stone the dog inert on the rug
Sylvia chopping up greens on the breadboard
in the cool kitchen   sunlight spreading a syrupy yellow
film a chemical bloom on the cedar wall

reading Seferis   poet of broad assumptions
steeped in art in centuries . . . a naked motor
sings like a doomed invention. . .

Emily Carr looking at trees for the first time
with "naked" eyes — a fiction of now
and disease of life confronted with objects
and syphilis as the naked man of the
rain-forest — a god who sits and looks at nothing

IDENTITIES — soothing unnerving part of the
trust of our time a past no matter how removed
although my feet (absurdly paired and
brown as polished wood) continue to build
their solid existence. . . "experiments — no (Picasso)
I saw it the way I feel at the time"
which is of course identities again . . . a

faith if you like for the ferry's loaded cube
(intent on exposure or stardom) squeezing
its liquid brilliance through a shoreline maze
or even these feet — numinous peanuts varnished tips of
some purple and yellow clearly-invisible Everest

SIQUEIROS

no hay mas ruta que la nuestra he wrote
dictating our future with
that terrible drive of his. . .
        in the Preparitorio
singing likenesses striding down
and out through the past
chanting pallbearers planting
the martyr's seed of tomorrow's world
mystical workers heroic overtones
of comradeship and vigour

later it's the liberty cap
    * Nueva Democracia
triple fists of dogma
breaking the chains

*This mural was painted with pyroxylin over cellotex covered with
cotton cloth. Modern tools and an active composition was again
applied.

triple threats of ducco
                    and
closed inside a bourgeois home
Cuauhtemoc Against the Myth

it's true he was intensely pale
the nostrils in his pictures were
no exaggeration

Sanchez bitterly —
he thinks he'll live forever
he might   his grandmother
died at 112

historical rectitude means opting
for eternity means constant striving
after progress   questionable labours

the proletarian clanking of the streetcar
heading for the Zocalo
catching sight of the Bellas Artes
feeling his presence
knowing he was there

RIVERA

the courtyard of the National Palace
a mirror for the vanished
solar gods of both cultures
the dangerous chill in the soldier's urinal
in the shack on the roof
running our little pounce wheels down
the black veins of the "cartoons"

a season passed
with our backs to the light
facing the fresh white plaster
our elbows on the balustrade
no word from the maestro
ailing it seems

ten feet off the ground
placing a chair under Rivera's settling backside
bulging blue serge suit with
white thalidomide hands

watching the two together
refining an editorial
quiet and deferential
abdicating in the rarest sense
Trotsky's body between them
the nascent body of a Mexico both
more and less than they'd bargained for

note on Siqueiros   revolution like form should
                      be spiritually biodegradeable

note on Rivera   in the evening under a single cup of
                      light   embossing indenting the
                      forms hour after hour   more like
                      a meditation than a gathering
                      synthesis

BETTY GOODWIN IN VANCOUVER

your objects declass you
in the only true sense
            for an artist
art is truth because it is
            BEING
            celebrated

        "sometimes. . ." you'd start
nervously gesturing
                almost possessed
the Chinese felt your obsession
                UNPRACTICAL WOMAN

    the Haidas
                would call you
        Trembling Hat
        give you a mat
                        half in terror and
                        half in humour

        the Goyim find you expensive
    a first or sixteenth sense
        enclosing a
            blind exquisite appetite

CHANGE UNCHANGE

often now
it's like
        something I feel
        through a glass

  the
sheets have that dreamlike
     white solidity that
beautiful ridged improvisation I
once lay down to live in

         your naked back
         (colour indentations)
    a miracle
  each time I see it
           stroke it —
    crest of affection
    sexual pain

a
  non-escape I now break
   into royal pairs

    touch your matchless centre to
    my circles of concern

CANADA DAY 1976

clearly disoriented but in
a positive way   added help from
a superincontinent light burning
the hilltop to liquids
roasting a languid cover of summer clouds

                    our hunch is wrong the main
event is not at Queen Elizabeth Park
structures tremble with life and instability
a Chinese bride — oasis of clear decision —
some men in her party wearing outsized ties and
gloves like minstrels (as if we needed theatre)
whichever way I turn people pass me closely
flaring off like nervous script
as liquid feeling I don't know whether I'm
cold or hot or if my
fractured state is visible. . .

finally the Stadium
performers — flipping insects in a spoiling green
dancers cut out by the sun   the show
mismanaged creatively   every nationality taking a turn
on the flimsy plywood stage   every state of verve
composure inattention health encloses
them like the weather
someone sings *This Land is My Land* in
Russian or Ukrainian   simply
as if they meant it

outside the entrance gates   a
crescent strip of shade   I'm shivering
a woman selling weiners that pop in my mouth
like Europe   a bread I don't recognize   she
hardly sees me as her barbecue has burst into flames
I look for my friends   the space beneath the stands
is dark with competing cooking smells
hurrying back-lit forms   echoing voices and
footsteps   purging gestures eye transactions
arms breasts heads

the mid-waist roots of art
pressing frameless computations

TOWARDS SLEEP

the worst insomniacs are writers
huge audiences go by like Pacific storms
logging trucks with roaring barns for engines
a smoothly-fitted leather-covered motorcycle parked in the light
                                      is the end of expectation
on marginal farmland a season of unmarked snow shining and
shrinking with age is the art of a favourite movie repeating
                                      itself on television

DECEMBER 7 1970

the rain takes a loose grey form the shape of an air raid siren
                              and   simultaneously

there are seventeen poets grouped in a vehicle of disintegration
                                                      a hod

someone is speaking to a child tells it   be patient   be helpless
                                                      even

a red dog moves as in memory   mentioning each white room
                              in his census taking

ON THE PAINTING *PANCHO VILLA DEAD AND ALIVE* BY ROBERT MOTHERWELL

for myth the day you should
turn to a tourist Mexico
sun in place like
a worn-down peso

six bullet holes (or eight)
have been artfully blotted
his sightlessness is a rich surprise
a slick of ambivalent whiteness

           shades of a
"Beery" with blackened breath
stubble   a mass that
laughed at the Virgin
cherry marbles flicked to the
crude child's circle of his gut

has anything really died or
which one officially lives
Motherwell shows in his lens
a passion of wasps   or shot-like
pores developing in the mind

spikes or legs for seeding the plot
where a leader might rise
immaculate and brutal

BROTHER LUC "FOUNDER" OF CANADIAN PAINTING

Brother Fix   ambulent Brother Luc
Brother Foetus of the Recollects
blessed   crisp in vocation   passed
like a spine of Text through the
stalled cumulus of lakes   a tufted cleaner
up the shining funnel
of the river   next in action we
also revive your mission
your gilding of cracks
your varnish of green pears

through a long ingestion
(centuries in fact)
base or passive positioning
trees loom out like
mops of seaweed   oxen   teepees
capes — the oil-snout of whales
the army with its unimaginative
requisitioning of scenery
sunday outings by the waterfall
the plodding fiddle of labour
thwacked into life —
a blue and red of the new land

remember the master painter Simon Vouet
maître of the allegorical
white front-face   Clouet's whirling
breast peeled from a royal fender
of cloth   the carnival barns of Pellan
stacked with roots and magic   visual clocks
and the swimming stares of humour

ON ARTHUR LISMER'S PAINTING
THE OLYMPIC WITH RETURNED SOLDIERS

a monument to the man himself
as iceberg striped by the world's
first crude form manipulators
cots in line like miners' trucks
reeking galleries abutting the dock   winter balm
an invention of this Sheffield expatriate
solids emerge character starts to dissolvle
                    and
I was there
somewhere beneath that first
hard-focussed funnel   held in check
behind deck-length fences of khaki
infants born   borrowed soldiers returned
innocent wives of a pivotal generation
                                    Lismer feeling
the tug of his painter's hands
checking his notes working from photos
(Olympic — a sister ship of the Titanic)
adding his sauce of fishboats willowy welcomers
soft progenitor hardened by freedoms
half in love with his art
half inclined to his dullard students

VINTAGE MOVIES

I'm beautified by the sentiment in vintage movies
innocence having crossed the Himalayas
I like the simplicity conferred on me by Viennese psychiatrists
I want my pleasures to blend with yodelling and laughing gas
I'd like to ski romance
with the style of Gregory Peck

I want a second steaming chocolate brought to my bedroom
                                                    door by
the blond and portly wife of the European innkeeper
I want her to smile her smile of complicity when I tell her
our bags are still in Milan   I want her to leave us to love
I want her to coach my girlfriend in rabbit stew

nobility having deserted the way it has
I want to be Gary or Rock at the tragic childbed end of Jennifer
                                                    Jones
and cry with my back to the cameras

MELVIN'S HAT

I was writing it Melvin
when Sylvia mentioned your hat
and it became the poem
remember Melvin's hat she asked
and down it dropped like a lemon into the slot
women have this awesome talent for instruction

remember Melvin's hat   sure I remember Melvin's hat
and I remember his mind and man's condition in the fifties
I remember Melvin's double-breasted suits
Melvin's shoes — I know — forever black
Melvin's girls Melvin's steady warmth Melvin's cross. . .

like some of those attitudes of yours you
wore it too much and certainly wore it too long
the sweat stains on the outside band
(it's not me who's complaining it's her
she says her father hid it at our wedding reception)
instruction again and thoughtless propaganda

but joking aside and as it's sucking the blood
of that earlier poem
I suggest you get someone else to write. . .
mythologize the thing

THE ANIMALS OF MY CHILDHOOD

the animals of my childhood
are the absent animals
of happiness and obsession
I remember one great horse
trapped in the snow and there
was a beautiful silver dog who
kissed me and died of a broken
leg elephant was a big word
that I hammered out of iron fingers
and in my own slight way
I was grateful mother and father
were basketweave and tabloid
nothing ate through the shell
of my settling pond the stillness
that pored me under the windows
properly naked and pagan was neither
bloodbeast shaman or love
the animals of my childhood
would have to include the ten
fingers in the bathtub the sheets by
the year whose weave and eyes
were dearer than my grandmother

MOÏSE PAQUETTE

at the edge of
          the Great Depression
                    Moïse Paquette of

the baseball cap
          (the garage owner and
                    district bootlegger)

joking it up with
                    my father on the
                                    lost St. Lawrence (blue

strip facing the Arctic)
                        while his cross-
                                        eyed boy of nine

(adopted they said)
                    filled up the Marmon
                                        from a tall mesh-

wrapped   cylinder   of
                        distilled   cranberry   juice
                                        "mornin   Chas!"
                                                        yes

we knew the routine
                    my mother defining
                                    her isolation my

father's face at play
                    (at work?) like a
                                Sun Mask   wooden
                                                    houses

strung along the poor
                        powdery grass   a
                                    chain of seaweed-

coloured rocks   the sky a
                            soothing oblivion
                                            like silk

indulgent enormous
                    listening
                            as we did

DAY OFF

my day of rest today
                  I need more sleep
                                 no words

TATTOOS
            Fine Original Designs by
                        Doc Haggis

no sign-collecting
                no taking of notes
                              that old

lumbercamp cook again
                    I run into him at
                            all times of

the day
        and everywhere
                  (discussed Melville was it

or Pound)
            don't think why
                      what he does in

that bank is probably
                  a wordless transaction
                            a little

crazy perhaps
           high bloodpressure
                    so far so good

bank pictures who says
                what's to be hung
                        a Winslow Homer

BREEZING UP
           children sailing round hats
                      knee britches

AMERICUNS
        a sky that's seriously
                beautiful

Gaugin a travel
         picture of Tahiti before
                travel pictures

Cezanne mostly water
           long plane of the water
                  telescoped

by blue
      the dynamics of the shore
              L'Estaque as it

actually is

LAST TANGO IN PARIS

opens up
      IN PARIS
movie maker's artful
           culture climate
      posing for réalité
Gallic order
       metric fortune-fevers
            measured
     by the
height the level
       size and ease of
         WINDOWS

peach and
        oyster-coloured glass
                grey-green
blue-grey stone
      METALICIZED
    an
aging vengeful
      ARCH-AMERICANO-GOD
            walked
or walking
      under sentence of the
          METRO ELEVATED
packaged darkness rattled
      into Passy
        curls to strike
like foetus
      degradations made with
           sex's
  limber thunderbolts
crinkle-headed Venus as
      maternal
      ARCH-ETERNAL-TARGET un-
comprehending Judas girl
      an able
        uninitiate
curled-up hate
      UNCURLING
uprights in
      an ocean-blue of focus
         moving into
empire blight   lovely
      bourgeois mausoleum
foetus in a corner
      of a culture-blighted
        MADHOUSE
balconies to life
    or
overtones of this
      and paranoia

BOLOGNA

                                as advertised
                                                (arcades bring

rain
        to my imagination)
the Square
                a mass of backsides
                                        the citizens a-
glitter
            know their roles in
                                tragic status quo
                                                    I
eat pasta
            wine beneath a
                                martial tower
meaner angle
                            BILLBOARD
on the bricks
                forty victims of the
                                        Nazis   some too
young
            quilt of photo-faces
                                    grey and black as processed
no repeal or grandeur
        Beatrice d'Este
                            resident in crime
                                        moat a noose
of light   lock of
                        pop proportions
trees of hunters' green on
                                wash of
                                        blue malar-
ias as advertised

MAYA

in classical times
               (the world supported
                            by the four Bacabs)
                                    in the
year that started
              with I Imex O Pop
                      the priests are parading in
force in pectorals and
               cloaks buccal masks
                        attended by
                            rattles and
outsized trumpets dancers
                  disguised as alligators

Incense flails its blue
                  experience faith is
                        voided from the
                            white
entrails of the conches
                athletes puke in
                      fervid exhaustions
                          the
artisans strain from
               their pen in the
                    fourth barrier The Lance
is held in a
         false gold hand by a personage
                    infinitely noble

all the paths have been
                beaten and redefined
                    for the fete of I
                    Imex O Pop
vegetable head-dresses close
                on the cross-eyed boy
                        who lays
                      his staves
across the calculations
              in an angle of caution women
                        fussed
                        and

ecstatic   in   a   square
                          outside The Square merchants
                                                        groom-
                                                    ing their patron
Ek Chuah

there is no horn rubbing
                          louder than another
                                                    danger slaked
                                                          to lengths
in the cooling lime
                          rhythms brass in intention
                                                    suicide is
                                                          represented
the stele of weaving
                          the heretic unit of leap year
                                                    royalty by
                                                          rumours
of jadeite   the jungle by
                          its splits of birds
                                                    medicine by
                                                          serpentine
                                beads as moist as cherries

the felly of the sun with
                          its three optical bands

JOHN LYMAN

1

luxe calme et volupte
an option that now   .
seems slightly reduced
if preordained   an image
refined in daylight
ripe civilities. . .

he took some pride
in the fact
that his feet were small
he laid out his palette
like a druggist which
his father was. . .

no Yankee cousins
Canadian foreigners in France
his solitary neighbour deep in
the spreading continent of art
was inaccessible
                    1907
the bourgeois summers rolled on
gathered unnatural sweetness
the art professors worked
at their blossoming charts
dabbed with classical measure
cut with magical vigour
a single
projection

2

I met him almost by chance
(my sexy aunt who worked on The Star
"of course I know an artist"
and she did)

in Montreal
          I remember
the faintest echo of Cannes in
Senneville (a place he knew well)
a harbour much too muscular
for Marseilles-Toulon
a number of long straight streets
on the east side of the Mountain
which could have been France
'under a blizzard of flags'
a river flattened by farms
graceless table   surplus serenity. . .

I still revere his icy
"Grier your fly is open"
an evening of tenuous depth   integrity
there was even a "Legion d'Honneur"
and I was seventeen
and had painted my first real picture
an authentic Arab a
Beothuk I wore his art
like a jellaba
tracked my innocence about

3

but what did I see
what do I really know
that isn't statistical
other-researched or second-hand
he was born in Biddeford Maine
(a link in the Connecticut connection)
at three his mother died

father   Frederic Gold Lyman
unmated layman of success
spaceless architect of springboards
LYMAN'S DRUGS   before my time

'even before the flattest
Quebec landscape I feel more. . .'
he wrote in his diary   1927
coming home to Montreal
ah the miserly stale
humanity of being "French"
the rootless monied sickness of "English"
ankle-deep in the good grey slush
we stood our ground
(waited you could say)   flinched like
plants in the
clear enamels of cold
summers of tropical closeness

4

1909
he found Matisse like
someone catching a stationary train
at the last moment
he and the Britisher Mathew Smith
were late comers
the convent converted to art
was in the hands of
Swedes and Germans
Europeans   polished   young   rich
exclusive. . .

colour serenity beauty
values pushed to the limits of
taste and rationality
mind and senses in ecstatic proverbs
imperial configurations
Le Dejeuner   the table as altar
La Danse   esthetic vertigo

Grande Nature Morte aux Aubergines
sensation as myth
intelligence as colour
  colour as transcendent order

AN ANTI-IMPRESSIONIST LANDSCAPE

why shouldn't I
admit it   it's
the pinhead lights
of the arbutus   the chalk
the bone of the man-made
cliff   the metallic anguish
which might be blue from
a lesser angle
it has its masters
everything has
it isn't exactly threatening
but *there* with
buckshot   blackness   shine
like holy silvers
a fastidious complexity

AUGUST WEATHER

no lightning and no mosquitos
just the full black forms coming in
their own numbers their own time
the weather we say

skies can be anything we like
simultaneous operas in the four directions
the touchstone of passive relief   buttocks light and dark
the scale of our daily bread   a daydream
that nobody really lives through

but their cleanest slide is not the word for our wisdoms
or the wordless feeling of heartbeat the teasing whiteness
in which stillness and motor unite

this has been a very particular summer
too much rain   no explosive decisions   too few wasps and bees
starving our sacred mountain of blackberries

dry as it seems these are important notes   gearwheels toylike and
                                                          basic
if that's all we need — our constant fear and acknowledgement

POEM FOR ROBSON STREET

one of these days my living inside your image
will have to stop   this cold October noon for instance
the streets releasing a kind of invisible black dishwater
an oily knee-high mixture of discontents. . .

the midnight dowels of your pupils   the skin-smooth smoke of
your constant affection. . .even that sex conversion — the putty-
                                                            grey
of your Grenfel jacket the scarf around your neck
half leaf half vision did you wash your hair? you didn't
so why does it look like NEW CREATION

this place as you know is earthquake prone
the whole damn coast running up north like a hardened scar is
where it could happen   institutions are crumbling — have
                                                    crumbled
the West grows fat for slaughter   Quebec yells *separation!*
like a psychopath in the Garden of Eden. . .

why don't you turn fanatical or evil?   couldn't you bring REALITY
(that poor bugger drugged and stripped to a mindless disillusion-
                                                            ment)
have him sit down as we eat here. . .talk — a judge a referee a
                                            taskmaster — a
fellow diner tasting the things we are — our glowing useless
                        vulnerable love — my unstable mania

WALKING ROUND THE SEA WALL   STANLEY PARK

so still today   almost a mystical experience looking
down into the milt-thick stare of the tide pools
coarse tobacco-coloured manes of seaweed on the saturated
                                                                  rocks
subaqueous moons all sizes blistered with tiny molluscs (visible
             diatoms) seal-black settings placer complexities

a stagnant weather system flooding its whiteness about us —
                                                          seeping
dove-core plugging the sun. . .a couple walking in wavering lines
                                                          young
confiding in their separateness   telegraphing harmony. . .Siwash
                                                          Rock —
a monument   abandoned phallus sprouting neo-phallics through
its fortress skin   eviction bird — a gull perched on the ledge of
                                                          its prepuce

the bridge ramp trussed from below balancing Renaissance
                                    brides on a treacherous
membrane or slick — a contour rocketing cleanly up and over
                       the pendulous lime-cheeked cliff
water lapping lipping the closest objects in its cancelling language
                                          or wavelights
something we might absorb or emulate knowing the present
                       state of our feelings. . .being
             miners masters of that future space — our
                                    narrowing dilemma

OPPENHEIMER PARK

at Oppenheimer Park on Powell Street
just up from the Double Happiness Food Store
vegetables on tables as they ought to be   the sky
stitched into the homely Vees of the bare branches

a space reclaimed by the emptiness of daylight
a no-man's-land where the saved or the blameless the
Baptist church the smooth ship's mast convene in
an orthodoxy of unspent violence   garlic and ginger —

matchless values together — forms between flower and root
a persimmon — shaftless top cupless acorn full complexion
of the goddess nobody sees nobody saw   McIntosh apples
(the season is late) glazed alizarin trucked to earth. . .

my hurt or theirs?   the warehouse is more like
a hermit's cave — a single mystic some crates as his
earthy essentials   the girl with the tragic nostrils still
spins freely in space   Chinese "black and white" is
hopeful after all. . .a man with crinkled hair who pinches

fruit as some recovered gold — invented fatal substitutes

POEM FOR SYLVIA

how can I say this freshly   crack the words' black mirror with a
                                              new vibration —
I find you awake absorbed planning a day of work
I love you so I put my hand on your naked breast instantly
                                              becoming its
       delicate rise its floating texture its seminal warmth its symbol
                                              its tactile oblivion
a pure deliverance a lie in the reach of worlds (which it is not) a
                     craftsman's tool a part of the morning. . .
how to explain — sailing that afternoon   becalmed in the dead
                              centre of the Sound
everything fallen away   subordinate   the city the names of its
                     beaches mountains country horizon
our boat erect alive on a milky imbalance of light   renamed at
              centre stage its masthead piercing humidities
'we've all come out of the sea' (as only you could say) going di-
rectly to the GREAT CLICHÉ that is our mystery and our love

EARLY JULY

early July everything parched and docile in
the still focus of the sun   slightly off track I'm
reading D'Annunzio's *To a Torpedo-Boat in the Adriatic*

how many skills interlocked — riveters
welders   machinists   electricians   boiler makers. . .
so much ingenuity   science   technology
turbines — almost silent power giving the thing
its visible extra thrust   macho-hysterical image

women   farmers   miners   ordinary labourers   generations of
slaves   ages of careful growth for a
military toy like this

art with a stained-glass wing of decadence
high falsetto of criminal boyish singing
a master of sensation   sick combinations
bombast beauty   dirty old poet of war-romance

BLOCK

there is no possible way of computing the damage
the trees are enormous spearheads of implacable coarseness
the mountains a distant frieze of puritan grandfathers
prophets in the snow-bib beards of their cosmic pronouncements

my feet are far too small and pointed for the job of walking —
the work of changing the scene   some great unkindness shines
on the plot of my striking perceptions — a desert parched
as tin   enclosure by wires finer than nerve connections

in every night there are thirteen ways of discussing the dead
bones of fish but only the single hope the adit that funnels me
down again howling into your life   flailing into the heartless
freedoms and beauties   the lacquered sprawling extensions

POEM IN OCTOBER

I

please love
protect
old photos
were we
this so solid
flesh of
another time
love assassinates
as do bullets
I see
does Venice fit
the man
(unkind contraction)
Prado hosts my
flapping trousers
topcoat cut
without flair
                free of
stasis flooding
the attic the
viewrooms
                then

II

trackless
scrambled from cars
striding off
plateaus
caperers
masterly squatters
sniffing positions
splintering
sun-logs
melting the pot. . .
we must turn
out sleeves of

what we've seen
cover trees
with
brilliant washing
bold recoveries

III

SAN MIGUEL ALLENDE

looked up at
the town is earthy
hunkered terraced
and down
felicitous and humble
roads sneak up
through freakish greens
then streak to
day-hole centre of oasis
sun a root
of blue   the sky a
slick a fender over
flaking pens
orchids   mind-smells in
abandoned tanneries
tourist junk in
courtyard pores (three
tiers for ruling)
diamond stones for
striking out
a revolution
                    if
history moves
then here
history moves backward
status quo   faces
smoothed by sunflash
from every angle
saints have passed
(Siquieros   Tamayo)

their presence erased
names proscribed
increasing our disbelief
Allende —
try to imagine his
loaded acts   the
costume if you can
the sash perhaps. . .
    and
the teacher from
Guerrero
Lucio Cabañes
dynamited they say
when the pay of
the "federales" was
doubled
   that contrast
made me real
that I do still
feed on the
dead horse past
the border   huge
nursing corpse   scarabs
of decay cupped
in my hands
emeralds for the
last conquistadores
the strangest
ones

IV

cricket-slaps not
dossiers   photos
are unstable
documents
blacking bias
focused in
absentia
   cached

in curtains   stripping
slats from
sacred monoliths
smoothing fibre
into
billboard flatulence
stalled expression
smile
only two projections
for the set-piece
(yours excepted Reva
yours excepted)
silent movie ace
or anarchy

V

if epic is demanded
then epic is
ourselves outside
ourselves
has scale is
metaphor
is damned unsmiling
time in every
man and woman
sweating in the
artwork of a fact —
survival
          modeling our
broken-backed moralities
and such
            is
clutch of friends
performing choice   unmatched
rocket-sculptures
striding out
of frames

stillness like
this caving stretch
of beach   your liquid
message   tilt
of breast
the unseized past
the loss of you
completely loved by
what you are

MY COUNTRY MY NONCOUNTRY

we are a people
Preoccupied
snowed under by others
loved by what we hate
moneymakers in a careful way

we shift and split the
icy incisions of region   the ghosts below
are more than we can bear
less than we can write about

the wilderness is ours   the
mounted goose rides out our dreams
of comradeship   a brutal heritage of
booze and business
confrontation naked as the paylands

we are conscience-heavy   drugged
givers in the sense of folding our arms
soda-suckers in the joy of
other cultures
                such reserve
has all the heart of storage
such unease makes cold a
stray amongst the wolves
space that gap of passion — crossed
appeasements looming at our backs

THE NATIONAL DREAM

the smoothly tailored rails

bags of detergent steam
released like parachutes from
a dragster

black as a hearse the engine
rocks through accordian space   then
like a tightrope walker
crosses the trestle bridge
stops backs up
crosses again. . .

Lake Superior   granite and shell-clear sky
(we alone the source of its cold)
horseflies   brown   clinging
like burrs to the sweating flesh
of the work-gangs

2.

in the beginning was what?
Ghea the Earth
Uranus her husband the Night
Chaos as Space both inside and
                    outside the envelope
pictures of some magnificence
man and his cosmic personifications

under the vertical pressures
we had created a new theogony
God the Timekeeper God the Boss
God the Queen is puffball-headed multiples

the Graces in descending order
                    accomplishment
                    wealth
                    frugality of the spirit
                    contentiousness

3.

having grown out of this dream
we've found it again at the bottom of our closet

the mountains are the still white gale
that lasts for the length of a meal

the lake is an abstraction as life contained
a lagging resevoir of time
a book with the single word   MID-AFTERNOON

like worms the segments grow but are not enough
their food has renewed itself   the rumble behind the hills
has been lapped by a cooler proposition

1885 — a man emerges with eyes like recycled oysters
the taste of a Cuban cigar becomes indelible
1886 — a second man with an air of failed disgrace stands
with his wife on the
cowcatcher of a slowly cooling locomotive

a national crest
a strict and hard achievement
a quick morality for Canada

THE CITY SAN FRANCISCO

the city has its native animals
some of them are beautiful
very hard and free   this
is their grassland

its comedians if they remember at all
have found that money is
a dead ground for humour

mugged at the steepest of hours   its
tragedian sings of the totally uncensored
only the dream of a tourist
is disturbed

kindness out of gear cuts flesh
across a thousand stenciled smiles
popping in the street lights   and as
the rituals prescribe   sex shoots
dryly from the hip

no one frees the barker   the
taxicab which blathers smoothly
into forepaws   it remembers fenders
like the jowls of
Texan presidents   if it
remembers

PROSE OF A FILM TRIP ON THE TRANSSIBERIAN RAILWAY

the largest computer   the ubiquitous atom smasher

generators housed and rooted like bulbs in the glassy river

grey as mist the paper factory with its tall crematorium stack

a "Stalingrad" truck swerving to cross the steppe between ridges

twisting flats the fiery sides of the railway cars   passengers' profiles

   close-up human fragments looming like level-crossing bells in the
                              narrow corridors

tentative leisure   tentative beach   tentative bathers dressed in the pure
                              democracy of

a Soviet mail-order catalogue   in the ant democracy of occupation as an
                              ultimate value

in the cold democracy of Soviet higher education

in the hard auto-dictatorship of man's impertinent science   imperial
                              technology

CYCLE

when I was five my smile of innocent pain my smile wider than a circle
was stretched on a frame of bird bones

when I was nine starched cocoons   cramps and couplings   heart-race
frozen on a winter sky

when I was twelve the sun burned everything white except my eyes

when I was seventeen I hung out the aura of women in sixteen shades
of yellow dye

when I was thirty-five   snow fell out of the bookshelves   myth rose up as
a raspberry-coloured billboard

when I was forty-six I mortgaged significant pastures   pasted my manly

pinup on ancestral temples — blue-baked T-shirt   boneless limbs like
Shiva

when I was fifty-eight stillness blocked me with its arm of roots

which inflections had shaped the paling like neon fruit?

what cool juice could break the imprint on my face?

THE EFFECTS OF COUNTRY STILLNESS ON A PLAYWRIGHT AND AN ACTOR-DIRECTOR

(for Tom Cone and Jayce Van Der Veen)

it struck them like a slow hypnosis
a drug erasing the armed alertness of secret agents one piece at a time
the Peruvian rug (the playwright even remarked on its close sweet-glow
vibrations)
the actor-director retired   reading fragments of poems which dropped
his guard punched a loft of stars instead of promoting voices
one was — what can I say — all ingestion all specific gravity
the other a profile for scouring corners a beak for trimming the blurs of fat
caiman for herding the one-and-only Distortion into painful focus

BAUDELAIRE MEETS BRAUTIGAN

having turned left with
an image instead
of right   Baudelaire
finds himself on
Market Street in
far-west San Francisco
present (and all but
inciting this coming) a man
too gaunt to be young as
blond as the husk of sin
as dry and scaly as
life without remorse
says Baudelaire "bonjour"
(plums dropping from his
every letter)   "now Master
say it like it's at"
the man rejoins (rebukes?)
through limp moustaches
itchy birds for eyes

GARY SNYDER

like much of
West Coast poetry
pretentiously
unpretentious
                 it seems
the pilgrimage is
endless   the bark mosaic
never completing a cycle

monastery
meetings
cabin of the thousand peaks
a whorehouse where the
small-scale girls have all
the poignancy
of brainwashed slaves

glazed with spaces like
the whole Pacific
                    or
chipping rust in the
black snake-hole of
a boiler

on a freighter   in
another century
with Lowry

FOR THE PHOTOGRAPHER   REVA BROOKS

Reva those
priorities of yours
husband first

Ibsen would have
typed you a Leica
just to turn it
on that stacked morality
anti-life   he'd say

what an act
holding themes by
neck-scruff   twisting
Jewish scenes
from superstition
values out of boiling void

standing cocked and ironed
in the circle underneath
the sunlit one
                    or
seated while the basking
father-figure cuts
your smile   shades
the trees for glitter

HENRY MILLER ON TV

like Picasso you have
to get used to his size as thought
and size impresses Westerners
he wears a cap
and lives with women

he's a small man like a marmot
and his head's a Gaulish pierre gravée
a Vercingetorixs
an alderman of sex
he'd fornicate in public

whatever came unstuck
and he knows what it was a sharp
leviathan of words has born him through
affairs of unsuccess
Europe's culture is
a poison in the puppy's bowl
he knows that too

his life has human scale
and that's good his acts are inelliptical
they fail for him

as Mona failed he's the dog that
totes the shameless gift the talking messenger
who never arrives

ELTON JOHN

blind man singing
(and what do I know
about blindness)

blind man (almost blind)
pounding it out with
magic frozen paws
settled amongst the stars as
the sign of Man-Sound Man-Piano

switching his role
changing his light   becoming the
phoenix bird or is it the
bird that never flies
blinding erect and radiating fifedoms
in fern leaves of electricity

an unmanned planetary clown
(globes of white in
an abandoned automobile factory)
conducting the slavish song of
our tribal autobiography

moving it all inside
shooting his longing like
a black tongue into the
voices of others.

MARYA FIAMENGO   CANADIAN POET

imagine the presence of Tito's wife
and the firm conservatism of
order as the tribal martyrdoms of Europe
"biographies are my thing" she says
but in a clear hard sense her
country holds her in focus

DISCUSSING "GREEK DAY" WITH A GREEK WAITRESS

"you should have been there "she said" I've still
got bruises from the dancing
but the parade was better last year
— you remember the war in Cyprus —
there was this huge map
half blood!"

1937

this could be labelled
a night picture (a season
of dying and airships)
night in its aspects of bluish
tawny   astral and pressing in. . .

the clearing existed by virtue
of beavers or thirsty animals   crazy
settlers in their fright   a finger pressed
by one of the founding millionaires
the water endured as water
ignoring the summer's thaw
                              the ragged trees
as claimed by a solitary heron

Andy   the passion was in the sounds
the listening   awareness
                           the name
of the sin was innocence
Maria   it was beautiful   bacchanalian
Peggy   your body forms
at the edge of a pond
which had no edge
                       your mark
has made the tundra blond
                              and less
than permanent

CONFESSION

I didn't go to the war
I'd been a fanatical in-fighter for
art and ecstasy — religion if you like
in 1940 someone pulled a
card marked HEART out of my personal file
it was threatening   it said
hostage-taking has already begun!

my loves had more than accelerated —
escalated like a movie strip of all
the most fabulous seasons
tripping and sliding into
each other's magic-mirror preserve

                 in spite of the card
times continued hard for my enemies
it didn't change a thing except that
I sat on streetcar benches
with the sun coming up

I took a wife and
broke her with my treasons

ALLENDE OF CHILE   Time's "tribute" condensed

Allende savoured
    THE GOOD LIFE
drank scotch
played golf (the bourgeois yoga)

in addition to
his family home
there was (reportedly)
a hideaway
to which he took
cronies
and women
barbecued steaks for them

a casual dresser
turtleneck sweaters at work
turtleneck even in death
(reportedly)

a posthumous film (government sponsored)
shows Allende's imposing
wardrobe and shelves of
imported-foods-and-liquors

like Lyndon Johnson a
leaner on people
a hard man but
not a ruthless one Allende spent
most of his day
working
to work for the people is really a pleasure
he once said

grandiosely

DOCTOR DAVID SUZUKI

please fellah   doctor man   no
more Canadian softness
nomore smiles   and if you
can throw a frisbee (and you can)
don't make "wonder" a question

so you want us to know what
the boys in science
are up to   and when we know
will we then have status
as co-conspirators?
are there flowers in the lab?
we could be those   floating functions
of our one-time life

Brezhnev smiles   Stalin didn't — we
smiled for him
Wernher Magnus Maximilian Von Braun's was
not the smile of slippery Max but
that of a child with a magic toy
do weapons-scientists smile?

Carter smiles in earnest — smiles in
his sleep smiles while tying
his daughter's shoelace
probably smiles into tapes

say problem-solving is 'beautiful'
I really shouldn't object
talk backwards if you like
slash at your silent brethren
don't smile

AFTER HEARING FRANK SCOTT'S TV PLAY ON THE RONCARELLI CASE

(A POEM FOR THE ROMA RESTAURANT)

it's shameful but
I remember a different place
another crusade

we were campaigners too
whether drinking or swaying painfully
gratefully at the urinals

as that's where it begins
we could start with the food
ravioli — soapy sachets of pasta

spaghetti — white ceramic hemispheres
mysterious alive   Chianti my
introduction to an old art

I met Emma Goldman there
(a booth against the wall)
and as counterpoise my cousins

Andrew the one who sang   the one
who raged inside   the one who had
gifts and wisdom and who died

the one who dropped like moonrock
into Lake St. Louis then
surfaced flat in the morgue   without

a cause and mourners minus one

MY MOTHER

my mother doubled as
the ash of snow
her perfumes bridged the gulf

the eggshell colour of
each of her years
was always in question

though Irish violence
shadowed her in waves   swallowed
her when she dreamed
manipulated mirages
fringes of unfrozen wool

her touch was warm but
out of reach   her lover an
impossible objector
fornicator   keeper of the seal

her wish that it would end
was just a cord that joined
her fragile expectations and
her sentence as
serene projectionist

FITZGERALD IN CANADA

they were like holy men
their hairlines grew fine
they were carried indoors on litters
their cars sweated rivets
their skins the liquids of the moment

assistant directors of a film which
was playing in four lost capitals
haunted by games in Biarritz
haunted by casinos
with green-lidded eyes
haunted by windows like
blunt thermometers arched with cane

think of the past as a virgin stick
whittled into awkwardness
think of the bootlegger's chimney
as a clear glass rod
stirring the recipe

cast by a war their wives
crossed fingers in plunging beds
dreamed of fashion or heartbreak
their faces gutted with laughing
their bodies bearing the
bruising knot of one last day

BIARRITZ

Basque-land   oil sculpture of the barricades   your flatness reminds me of
                          the discovery of a remarkable cactus extract
the pitch of the dream excursion   Beaune   Beaune. . .
our coming through coastal woods reactivates the signs   coming by car
        ripping like cloth through gypsy relevance (a mockery that might
                          be understood a century from now)
I ask for the time and
when you say the casino is time the answer is right
when I ask you for the season you say the seasons have stopped and I
think of your name like the lustre and peppery bubbles of a fine
                                        champagne
anchored together with scarlet bolts the houses exhale   the streets sleep
                                        whiter than novels
we walk the beach and by noon our voices have swerved through the
        lost sand- drawings of Picasso   the scandals that rocked a Republic
                          and in which everyone played a role
and by dusk my shirts are all come back bluer than a seaward mile   filled
                          with freshness like mother's bodice
I ask you to light the candles (the biggest of all the rose-swirl)
to lay out the gears for another day
and the coupon books

GRANDFATHER

a size that's hard
to compress grandfather
Irishman   Florentine in
English Montreal
dispensing ukiyo-e prints
for this or that occasion
sunsets over sofas
Bernini's plaster "chase"
Hermes on the stairs pitched
on one talaria a
hot-dog god. . .

batchman   traveller
in drygoods   saint or
saintless immigrant your
future was the thing
a change of slides and
you're in paradise
Canada your fresco
seven children with florid
Edwardian names   a
wife of lofty innocence
a scientist for God
a trailblazer

your favourite dead in France
you vowed to keep in touch
fell back on the link
between occult and
the metaphysic of wealth
did it shake you
leave you more serene
league of black-haired women
Blavatskys groping for
your pocketbook   weaving
sharpness round your
geniality

when you posed at Luxor
as a sheik   when you graced
canoes as ballast
charmed enormous salmon
into your empire   did
something stain your ton
sting your vest
a claw unlatch your hat
to program boom then bliss
bliss then blindness?

THE RICH MAN'S SON

for the rich man's son
spring dies hard

but the animals
will close the forest to his dreaming
the bodies of women
firm out the wall of
their tendinous sisterhood

money is the edges of the square world
money is the eye that
drops from a speeding car
money is prize-winning thought   the jumbo loop
the enamelled frosting

there is Art for the rich man's senses
extravagances made in his name
order because he demands a change from
extravagance and disorder

there is the extra silk
of his special linings
loyalty's private decay   there is
the cold blue searchlight of his health —
a pin-stripe star
gigantic as Alberta

the rich man's son is white and firm
like a prophet's tooth   a niche can be made
to project this object
and to bear its smiling

FLASHBACK   LOWER ST. LAWRENCE

vertical fusion — fog and night
a masterful blackness
an Africa of weaving

a canoe with
a campstool in the middle
two of us paddling
one of us enthroned

the three-beat
circling beam of the lighthouse
carving a luminous block of
giant asbestos threads   holding
us in suspension
one of us enthroned
two of us working like demons
gibbering   Amazonian

at last a
grounding on stones
delirium subsiding   a neutral
reality talking of substance
darkly admonishing

voices calling our names
the lights of a car
round with anxiety
yellow with fear

FLASHBACK   LOWER ST. LAWRENCE

not really a place in itself
just high rock and a tree in
the centre of a field
we called the "island"

the railway was something else
bossed by a proper Irish widow from
her shady beach house built
before the town discovered beaches
fifty miles of track   three
recycled locomotives
wooden coaches   windows slipped
by straps for easy spitting

shovels cached at the "island"
to think (I think) we dug
a trench in the railbed just
at the crossties' edge
covered ourselves with blankets
when we first felt the trembling

held each other down
as the sun went black
the search became reality

wind of heated metals
                              grease
piston boxes grazing
slathering steam   breathing
victims like a minotaur

TALK

a different day
each time I take my
nose off the typewriter —
tender sunlight   rocketing greys
twittering bamboo

lunchtime — starting with salad we
switch to words seasoned by stillness
feeling and stillness
stillness and Art   stillness and fences
stillness   CONCEPTIONS
stillness   CONCLUSIONS

chewing becomes percusive   digestion —
a miner's lamp scraping its light
on narrowing blackness

just in time you stretch and reach
for a pencil   I go sniffing for water
a stone in my tense
performing throat   the room (our
master retreat) reverberates

my final words. . .and yours I hope
noise means pain
in most of the universe

FOR KATHY CERNAUSKAS

I often see you
hear you play
now I learn of your passion for screwdrivers
your short computer holidays

our talk about origins slyly
reforms about you
historical base as a mural grows bright
with collective absurdities
                              but
to put things straight Lithuanian
is classed as a Baltic language with
proto-Indo-European roots

certainly to be — or to have been — Lithuanian in
the mass declensions of our day is legendary
to be blond without jokes or confusion is
almost as far from Helen of Troy as it is
from Marilyn of Los Angeles

Birute your childhood name
became Canadian *Brooda*   you change it
the ancient hero who carried the Vestal
Birute back to his icebound homeland —
what he had there was
fire tended with proper care
(not like today)
the infant fire of culture the fire of the imagination
the individual fire that *does* go out

you stood with Alex against the hydrangea leaves
legs as tall and unique as sculptures (legend again)
blond in your own particular land of
daylight resignation (always holding the rigid snake
the melting chrome of your flute)
                              you said half joking
take our picture — please — before we get old

BIRD STREET

I'm living on bird street and
mind you I have nothing against bird watchers
except perhaps that they eat cows
when I was a child I'd watch a nun go by
tolling the black bell of her faith or
watch the grey-faced man talking of God and wonder
wordlessly how God had so utterly deserted him

there was more grace in the still glittering tops
of the four poplars in our yard   more echo when
my grandmother (she of the innocent "beautiful thoughts")
always managed to bump me or
knock against my budding private parts
angel woman life will remember you

weeds are also a threat because
I've claimed to thrive amongst weeds
books I've yet to read implore me
a poet from Taiwan rudely writes me out
discovering the undiscoverable —
my coded highways of feeling

frees himself from all retreat

I'm the stuffed one (the birds can fly)
stuffed by their merciless signatures   the hard
wavering of crows working against the wind
their rapid genuflexions out of sunglare
the burst and cut in the alders

it could be invisible mountains curving ever higher over
my roof   the cedars — troughs in the fire of vision
candles infected with size
intractable   unlit

YOUNG MANHOOD WOMAN IN A STORE ON MONTREAL'S GUY STREET

the store was a sweltering den of
body odour woman distress
when she finally realized my presence
she dealt with me blindly through
the thick luminous walls of what
must have been a raging fever
I felt a sexual awe for certain
"older" women like this one and
almost lost my head in those
sumptuous rancid emanations
I wanted to say something infinitely
kind and civil and I also wanted
to press my firm cool penis up
and into her centre drawing
the poisons away from that
fabulous-ordinary fever-shimmering goddess

BEATRIX POTTER MICKEY MOUSE

we've brought our
children up on Beatrix Potter
and Walt Disney — Mickey Mouse of the
high child's voice and the pure white gloves
a linear Beatrix drained transfixed in
the seventh veil of her innocence
tigers roar. . .or do they
grizzlies claw or are they
dancing giants rehearsing a commercial into which
we sometimes fatally intrude
the food chain — why did it grow so like a tree?
survival — why does it holler
BROTHERHOOD-VIOLENCE SISTERHOOD-JUNGLE
punching the tiny god of our morals   the order
that faith hangs up from bleeding palms — our sacrifice

RACHMANINOFF

old iceman
of sound
when I was five
we had lunch together
I said to you. . .no you
said to me. . .

and later that day
as you graciously
played *en famille* my uncle
let his crow loose

a blot on my clan
humour as black or
as sick as the
poor man's war-shot lung

in your pictures
your nose — so large and
it's said you
suffered from melancholy

each generation will
find your delivery —
blocked clear and icy
with colour
dissolving in time
like part of a day

its frailest strength for
times like these
that vertigo of feeling

RAVEL

through the wall to my right   rock-muzak
my candy-craving wife beating a pot
of fudge   the dog has
farted again — indescribable
a program honouring Maurice Ravel
L'Indifférent being sung by Maureen Forrester
neon concert image   the diva next door
near-perfection in a crumbling age

Debussy on Ravel   the flawless ear
a sick Ravel on himself   no more pleasure
in the making   I have failed
am second-rate. . .music as a language
this beautiful idea has used me
is inadequate—
              and incidentally a
tradition had popped up in France
of bourgeois tinkerers   engineers
in the new tradition of metals and gasses
invention as escape from
words and class and paper emasculation
and historical art
the father building his two cylinder motor
was the son composing music
both transitionists   both
preparing for flight
nomads   lightweight glidermen
                           ornithopterites

REMBRANDT

it all seems too familiar
the rich man Six pulling
selfconsciously at his beige gauntlet
the scholars (moralist man)
as indispensable then as our
present-day ideologues God help us
the floors as polished as mirrors
the syndics sensitive to their image
the air for everyone to breathe
only the painter is odd   his
clumsy charades his asses laugh in
the glass   a man who travels
might be the last to find him bearable

a miller's son who might have been a
jurist or a divine had he the mind
or the pretentions   a linguist
inventing his craft
a mother's boy deep in the mine of an
inward personality (this is a guess) eschewing
plateaus of light   the clear or the cold
white faces of the master Caravaggio

his life was to paint what he was   intelligent inward kind
awkward immersed   outlasting with blind integrity
the vital drift of his times   the ones
who could serve him best
Saskia dead in her baby fat   Hendrickje struck
like an amateur coin
Titus whose fever and light ignites the air

ZURBARAN AND VELAZQUEZ

their brilliance as painters
aside Velazquez was a
potential cinematographer while
Zurbaran was the fixed eye
the television box of
his day   for him the black
and white spectrum of authority
was as cool and innate as
a Stalinist purge
celebration of life
drained backward into
scarified flesh into wood grain
(Gris was only 300 years
away from his master)
with his Household rank Velazquez
was on joking terms with
his blundering patrons
noting monstrosities with
urbanity   setting the chambers
and chamber-pots as the court
decreed   one was mindless then
and the other urbane
both agreed on accepting
the smooth-faced nobles and
bishops who drove at
their tortures as other
men drive at their wives

ROSSO FIORENTINO OF FLORENCE (1495-1540) AND
FEDERICO BAROCCI OF URBINO (1528-1612)

between the work of Rosso
Fiorentino and Federico Barocci
was the difference of murder to
sweet stagnation   Barocci's
Christ in *Nole Mi Tangere* is a
shampoo salesman demonstrating his
wares to The Magdalen a
discouraged aristocratic housewife
the barn siding fools no one and
off in the distance
golden buildings blowing away
like straw   Rosso tried
to outflank his masters but all
he left were typewriter eyes and
mouths ajar like the
toothless slot in a pillbox

THE ELEPHANT CELEBES

for Max Ernst

hope has lost a friend
as spaceman's engine failing falls
in yaws of kerosene-black smoke
a celebrant's descent a
dreamer's near catastrophe

a huge inflation called the
Celebes leans against the afternoon
sky between its legs
vacuum hose for sigh   and
one that plots its path
a headless nude for docking

metals ride the high
encampment of its back   squatters
knife-voiced warriors through sunblack

canister with two-step in its flange
a puff of boiler air
its name implodes
and leaves a mooring mast
a stripped caduceus
to sing to

ON SEEING THE JACK BUSH EXHIBITION

'the five colours blind men's eyes'
and possibly for the last time and
from radically different quarters —
innocence maintained in
a double armour of
unclaimed land and leisure
that bland coincidence

how else could we distill beyond
inference beyond reference
jam the sages   hang brocades
as if they were courtly riddles
filleted lockets splayed and
locked in gaunt museum glass

like everyone else I face the
smothering surgical changes
fine minds layering the
still sunlight of feeling
the child's myopia   I understand
that we must sift and energize
analyse and name. . .

lava like perfect iconoclasts
probe the paradise turning against
our rapacity. . .hold the cry
unseen in our throats
spiral back to the rock-lit tones
of our critical deeds

JACK BUSH

Jack Bush has died
in the flux of
a deep-glow sunset I read
the scandalously insignificant notice

thought of his elegant white hair
and of the time we
stood together and stared
at ragged patches of colour
on naked illustration board

if he'd been a hijacker
or a politician
or an American media star. . .
but then we'd never have
looked the way we did
at what we saw

the way no other generation will

USING IT ALL

using it all
the sound of Greek
cachectic *kakhexia*
that first hard thump
into daylight on
the garden swing

constancies like a smooth night's sleep
the comfort of foods
an endless burrowing into the
bright lives of others
the touching of skin on skin

one man's war in the lanes   in
the shadow of apple trees
in the grids of the human condition
both mindless and mind-imprisoned

the stars of one's parents
the stars of the mysteries of art
the convict of guilt
burnt to ashes by colour

the vision of strain and utopia
a constant equation
the prayed-for plateau
the prayed-for and rabid
proliferations

THE SOLITARY ARTIST

you can become paranoid
the solitary artist
becoming more sensitive — nothing responds
and sound stops like
blackness in a horn when
you raise your paper all intact anticipating
sweet cross of the muse

morning has failed your test
the first light has been warped back
into its box like a broken tennis racket

at your window leaves display their differences
opened hands   spread-out samples
you do not write for leaves

they wait to be moved while you
put your weight to
the fractious ball of your "Vision"
angle the urgent missile
whose centre has cooled
like a dead planet

THE TIMES

a sign of the times
my artist wife has started to dream
of trade union contracts instead of
abstract infinities

just this morning (I'm half awake)
Elizabeth Taylor makes a movie
with scab-rous actors and actresses
not exactly the "meek" or the "earth"

in fact the peak of absurd idolatries
and the sadly merging shadows
of what solidarity?

to restore her natural imbalance
I tell her *The Stone-Breaker* (a proletarian
masterpiece by Courbet) was destroyed
by Allied bombs in Dresden in spite of

fastidious Nazi protection and total
Communist indifference   nothing I say   is
what it seemed when programmed
or explained and the dream subconscious —

a children's garbage pail   a clumsy table
for her flights of plastic language

TRIP TO PENTICTON

easy access from
the myriorama   seven choices
mid-day with a glider moving
slowly across the
steep green mountainsides
grasslands   a slaughterhouse intensity
the drive-in at Keremeos as
flimsy and contained
as a space station
nobody talks much in B.C.   it
worries and confirms
us as humans   leathery skin
a too-ripe mouth split to the teeth
the commune baby
healthy with fever   screaming

FLYING WITH TONI ONLEY   SYLVIA AND SUSANNA

1.

climbing up from the Sound to Garibaldi Lake
over the sad intestinal winding of logging roads
straight over mountain ridges with sheer
impossible drops like the cliffs in dream suicides
the airplane — what an invention smooth then
sluing gently bumping gently in an element
flowing and wavy like summer heat
Toni bearded (an English engine driver) reaching
up for something he has to pull or press
everything spiralling upward in the noiseless
saturating noise the women's exalted voices

2.

the north slope of the mountain peak   snow with
a steeply climbing herringbone of short stabbed crevasses
clear flat islands of tone (Lawren Harris' cosmic peace revisited)
the animal grey of the moraine so uniform that
shadows appear to be charred tree stumps

ANSWERING JOHN'S LETTER for John Ivor Smith

we think of you so often John and
wonder (at least I wonder) if the Other is
still as inaccessible to you or if the
great lean Salmon sacred in its emerald pool of glass
lies just below my feet

we who made this world who believe in
what it does must answer questions
ask one John it might bring us that much closer
perhaps we could pool our insights and our doubts
become the new elite society of three

there are murders in Quebec there are murders here
right now Monique Leyrac is singing through that
clear sad sound of hers. . .with a flute accompaniment
she seems to bypass our thought and irony
lie in the gut of life lightlessly is

that the answer how *you* could sing
bawling a chorus from *Roll Out The Barrel* with
that dead look in your eye jaw working stiffly
like a ventriloquist's dummy
"fun" you'd bark and all its resonance gone
the word would drop like a baker's nightmare

snobbery of course but something else something insoluble
you against the world hilarious and parallel
anguish spent or emptied at your birth the only way

PAULINE OF ST. HYACINTHE

High from Down East! —
     I've fallen in love again the
               last three months. . . !
like me announcing —
master poems on the way!   I've done it again —
     everything out of my life except for perception!

(despite her age) *after several weeks of*
     living with him am still convinced I
               want to live alone!

     it's never simple of course
     wasn't it I who wrote
                         O artist beware
                         The saintly family life,
                         The Sunday of destruction,
                         And the insect death

     black-haired female VAMP   you I
       feel could revive your precious "love"
               in a tiger's gut
             Holy Daughter of St. Hyacinthe
           grow lillies out of
             inner-city murders

VANCOUVER EAST CULTURAL CENTRE

my god where am I? in the Soviet Union?
the bad old reactionary Ukraine?
nobody's throat cut   O.K.
onion domes for supper that's my trouble
I must have been here before
up the hill   wooden houses   night   rain
a movie landscape remembered
Maxim Gorky? who cares   it might explain
the oldness in everyone's smile   the
feeling of winding down   the corners   the
revolutionary blackness under the balcony
Max goes by   Max what century are we in?
the dancers come out and miracles begin
music clips at the dark like a parrot machine
an anti-static tongue   a life enforcer

DOCTOR ZHIVAGO

it's close at the movies
hot as a summer in the Urals
bodies around me peeled from their coats
everyone and no one

"buildings are political"
a girl on my right
she argues   her boyfriend disagrees
I make a survey for her   instantly
declare the country bankrupt

Zhivago centres the darkness
a puppet face of love and
privilege   a poet too
it's hard to believe a poet
on Denman Street and utter silence
not even the crushing of
a candy wrapper

                then to
the cold and the suffering   the
iron treasons of Russian life
one side bleeding the
other till someone gives   the poet
next time the tyrant
the heavy policeman finally
dropped to his knees

Zhivago and nobody coughs
Zhivago   nobody stirs   Zhivago
in the terrible wonderful snow-glare
Zhivago liking the ambiance
of his writing table

the broken Zhivago white and queer
in the resurgent city
amongst the lunch pails

the lights go up   hands on
my knees I ponder the question
is poetry political   heavy moment

out on the street I'm unnerved by
this Twentieth Century
soviet of skyscrapers

BERGMAN'S *THE PASSION OF ANNA*

in *The Passion of Anna*
Max Von Sydow is the HUMAN ISLAND
we can share his choice but
can he

the cruising camera catches
him treading stiffly off like
a spooked deer in
the snow of his yard

the colour's anemic and long
runnels mark his face for despair
he's brought kindness with
him and books   so what

out of island rock
under stationary grey
Evil's loose   lynching a beagle
crossing his path with
succuba (once women) the
vessels of love brimming with
love backed-up and stagnant

kisses exchanged seem tender
enough in the gas-white flush or
silhouetted on watery glass
sadness starts to drain

but what alas is turning man
against men   Eve against Anna
tugging on steering wheels
slaughtering sheep

raping the flesh
of snow   blazing like Fate after
the fire itself has offered
its own capitulation

PNE   IN PRAISE OF FAIRS

the fair is like an artist in heat
a poet expanding his word-landscape until he can say
"involvement" or "passion" or
whatever else he has in mind
    — Whitman carries you ten feet over the cliff then
       carries you back and starts again —
and even taken a bit at a time
the hard reality of something set to shake you scare you
take you or pour you out of a careful stance
    — behind the comic strip — the whip the crack the academic's
                                    despair —

the fair
the fair
the shock that doesn't pacify or cure
the surge that leaves you 25th to the winner
fireworks that say to feeling
we are the bang sweet highbrow if
you are the shivering element

POETRY

water from a hose—silver splattering cow pies
someone shovelling gravel—berries
rattled into the granary
the sugar-coated pill is mine not yours
'art is a form of intimate mental hygiene'
believe it or not the words of
an American poet   and ain't it the truth
and isn't definition a wonderful thing
my troubles are in the administration
                                   for example
despite my cousin's collection of early jazz
je n'ai jamais possédé le sens du rythme
the African message came too late
and badly supported
too much landscape perhaps too much kindness

my weakness for sensibility is of my birth
and of my times (a nudge from Grandma Society)
surface (for me)
the smooth unknown
the great magician's trick

a poet is not a messiah although
a messiah dies in every poem
he is
she is
the grocer of software   a priest of affirmation
a sensitive relocation machine

the medium is language
the first and most difficult rule because it humbles
esthetic detachment

QUEBEC

I wasn't expecting it and I don't exaggerate
but some recent poems of yours have brought
me back to life   turned me round and round
like a radar beam scanning
the soft blue tear-line of the mountains

I'm feeling your flexed components inside me again
a meal of candle-cracks   textures   tensions
longing that's poured its blood and waiting
into the mortified images of winter

someday soon your pressing songs may stretch and
sleep their night on a rockbank of stillnesses
stillness bearing the cuts of your fingernails
the ruts of parochial boredom   your whips

your three profound conversions. . .
laughter helpless with reverence and fever
fasting with a bright incontinence

2.

once in 'sixty-four' going back or forth on
yearly migrations within your borders I came
on a barricade of white words painted on
dark-age country paving   QUÉBEC LIBRE

my homelessness at that moment turned to yellow oil
the great neutrality in which I'd lived without
a single pact of communion turned its back
a word from the public cabal of language was now
worth more than childhood movies snoring genealogies

uneasy though I feel I wish you all success
your bishops in the past your "bishop" in the future
are more than a match for the spear-like arrow
(blue at either end) that fixed my morning dream
anchored tidal waves in simple contradiction

I can't forget you ever and how we both stole
sides of the same apple chewing it differently
living here "out west" with polygons instead of farms
wilderness in place of patriots   cities
that are chrome and sealblack   untouched flesh . . .
I'm turned to other confrontations   sometimes

see you slickly as the railroad Chateau set
against a sweet undreamed Tiepolo sky
which must be something missing something else if
we are (fractured or together) turning this to peace

UNTITLED

we need a
day of passion
a thick parade
of animality
fertility of voice and leg
O ASHTORETH-ASTARTE

GAME FOR A NEW NEIGHBOURHOOD

looked out the window   played our game
what does he do
pomaded hair the white Cadillac convertible
it was almost too easy and
you were right
a gangster you said

one still night there were
tight pants out on the street
someone being kicked between Lincolns
the gangster's door was
lit like a laundry chute
call the police you said   now
wait said I   gangsterland is separate

he had sons and a wife   the
wife was a French Canadian comely and human
what does she do
rides herd on his call-girls
it wasn't a guess

his sons were like all sons but with
looser style   something extra and expendable
what will they do   we shook our heads

the gangster died   pushed
downstairs on Christmas Eve — in Bordeaux jail
sinister   a full investigation they cried
nothing further was heard

what do *they* do

MY BROTHER

my brother died
with a card in his hand
it had Spain written on it

his garden had the most
fabulous scents jasmine
moonlight laurel
you name it

it could have been his charm
or a hallucination or the
patient beauty of a certain place
at a certain time

two streets below the sea
came in like a sad mistress no one
had explained her to the rocks
the rocks would cut your feet

whatever happened happened young
there was sadness in his eyes
but this belonged to his death

his life was
wrapped about him like
a coat of bearskins
something warm at least
smelling of man

RAIN

it's raining individual drops
it's raining the long grey sparks of anxiety
it's raining nights and extinctions and warnings and shelters
it's raining a history called Women's Relief
it's raining the copper forms of skyscrapers and the passions of coffee
                    and the menus bursting into cabbage rolls
it's raining in the prints of Hiroshige in the memory of Majas in the
                    string-plucked oceans of Iannis Xenakis
it's raining into thickets on the Queen Charlotte Islands
it's raining Chinese proper names into the unpacific Pacific
it's raining Mondays and Tuesdays
it's raining up the city from its secret platforms
it's raining down the Revolution from its perilous marquis on the
                    Embarcadero
it's raining the souls of housemaids in unwholesome poems
it's raining games of darkness for the children travelling from A to B
it's raining Europeans who have mastered the rain it's raining Japanese
                    who expose themselves like film in its brief kimono
it's raining moss and mindlessness and surrenders
it's raining down the ladders of wasps and the life form of trees and the
                    privacy of seeds
it's raining on boxes and roof tops and murders and fountains
it's raining on the trunks of stampeding elephants
it's raining on the Great First Digit buried in the middens of Mount
                    Vancouver